Complete Instructive Manual for the Bugle, Trumpet and Drum

Also from Westphalia Press
westphaliapress.org

Complete Instructive Manual for the Bugle, Trumpet and Drum:

Signals and Calls for the US Military Service and Boy Scouts' Service

---

by V. F. Safranak

WESTPHALIA PRESS
An Imprint of Policy Studies Organization

Complete Instructive Manual for the Bugle,
Trumpet and Drum: Signals and Calls for the
US Military Service and Boy Scouts' Service
All Rights Reserved © 2017 by Policy Studies
Organization

Westphalia Press
An imprint of Policy Studies Organization 1527
New Hampshire Ave., NW
Washington, D.C. 20036
info@ipsonet.org

ISBN-13: 978-1-63391-607-4
ISBN-10: 1-63391-607-3

Cover design by Jeffrey Barnes:
jbarnesbook.design

Daniel Gutierrez-Sandoval, Executive Director
PSO and Westphalia Press

Updated material and comments on this edition can
be found at the Westphalia Press website:
www.westphaliapress.org

COMPLETE INSTRUCTIVE MANUAL

FOR THE

BUGLE
TRUMPET
DRUM

Containing the Signals and Calls used in the United States
Army, Navy, Marine Corps, Revenue Cutter, National Guard, and
Boy Scouts' Service, together with other information pertaining thereto

BY

V. F. SAFRANEK

BANDMASTER UNITED STATES ARMY

Price, $1.00
In U. S. A.

R

CARL FISCHER, Inc.

Cooper Square

NEW YORK CITY

Boston   Chicago

· CONTENTS ·

V. F. SAFRANEK

PREFACE · ·

The purpose of this work is to supply a complete instruction and reference book for Buglers, Trumpeters and Drummers in any branch of the United States Service. In order to make the work as complete as possible, some calls not in use at present have been included, inasmuch as they might again be adopted at some future time.

It has been the author's endeavor to embody all information of interest to the bugler or company musician, without constant repetition or statement of unnecessary and obvious facts that clog up the average book of this kind, and help only in overfilling the work with uninteresting material and confuse the student. The rudiments are here sufficiently explained ; the exercises for beginners are instructive, and only good quick - steps, inspection pieces, etc., have been used.

ATTENTION
IV

SOUNDING A CALL
V

SOUNDING A CALL
VI

INSPECTION OF BUGLES
VII

INSPECTION OF BUGLES
VIII

INSPECTION OF PISTOL
IX

X

ATTENTION
(The Position of a Soldier.)

Heels on the same line, and as near each other as the conformation of the man permits.

Feet turned out equally and forming an angle of about 45 degrees.

Knees straight without stiffness.

Hips level and drawn back slightly; body erect and resting equally on hips;chest lifted and arched; shoulders square and falling equally.

Arms and hands hanging naturally, thumb along the seam of the trousers.

Head erect and squarely to the front, chin drawn in so that the axis of the head and neck is vertical; eyes straight to the front.

Weight of the body resting equally upon the heels and balls of the feet.

THE HAND SALUTE

When this salute is made as a part of recruit drill, there are two commands, one"preparatory" *(HAND)* and the other of "execution" *(SALUTE)*. For the preparatory command raise the right hand smartly till the tip of forefinger touches the lower part of the headdress above the right eye, thumb and fingers extended and joined, palm to the left, forearm inclined at about 45 degrees, hand and wrist straight; at the same time look toward the person saluted. For the command of execution, drop the arm smartly by the side. When the salute is rendered without command, the first position is held until acknowledged, or until the officer has passed or has been passed. If uncovered, stand at Attention (Position of a Soldier) without saluting.

INSTRUCTIONS TO BEGINNERS

Before attempting to blow a note on the bugle or trumpet, the beginner should seek instruction from an experienced musician in order that the mouthpiece be placed on the lips correctly. Once the lips are accustomed to any certain position it becomes very difficult to make a change, and many good candidates compromise their future on instruments of this kind with a misplacement of the mouthpiece.

The upper and lower lips each covering one half of the mouthpiece is considered to be a good position, but care must be exercised to avoid placing the mouthpiece on either side of the center of the lips. Practice placing only the mouthpiece (without the bugle) gently against the lips and blowing tones on it, then, while blowing, allow the instrument to assume its proper position around the mouthpiece, then again withdraw the instrument, still continuing the tone on the mouthpiece.

Stand erect and always hold the instru - ment straight from the body, horizontally. Do not point the instrument down toward the ground as this position cramps the lungs and gives the performer a very poor appear - ance.

Some buglers believe that by using a mouthpiece not made for the instrument better results are obtained, but it should be remembered that the bore of the mouthpiece should conform to the bore of the instrument with which it is used Cornets, trumpets and fluegelhorns appear to the average performer as very similar, but their bore is quite different. the trumpet being cylindrical, the fluegelhorn conical and the cornet "betwixt and between." The bugle is more like the fluegelhorn than like the others, but it should still be borne in mind that the manufacturer of the bugle has made a mouth - piece intended for the instrument not for the lip. If the performer cannot play without some freak mouthpiece it is evident that he either did not get good instruction as to the placing of his mouthpiece on the lips, or he is not adapted to the work, and it were better that he expend his energies in some other line of endeavor in which his chances of success would be better. Silver plating the mouthpiece is heartily recommended.

The instrument should be cleaned internally at least once a week so that the saliva does not accumulate and corrode. For this purpose hot water is considered as best. A thorough flushing and rinsing should be given.

The mouthpiece having been properly placed there are three requisites that should always be kept in mind by the experienced performer as well as by the beginner a good tone, a good attack, and sustaining strength.

A good tone is acquired by the practice of long, well-sustained notes, beginning with the lower notes and following with the upper ones

as the lips get stronger. Care should be taken
to avoid tiring the muscles of the face in the
beginning, and the student should cease prac -
ticing temporarily at the first sign of fatigue.
These long notes are sustained as long as it
takes to count 24 or 30 in march time, usually commencing the note softly, gradually in -
creasing the volume toward the middle, then
gradually decreasing toward the end. The im-
portance of this practice cannot be overesti -
mated, though on account of its seeming sim-
plicity it is more often omitted than observed.
In a total of one hour's practice, ten minutes
should be devoted to these long notes. Take
breath through the corners of the mouth or
through the nose, not through the instrument.

A good attack (striking the tone)   is obtained by tonguing practice, of which there
are three kinds_ single, double and triple.
The first named is accomplished by a stroke
of the tongue as if the performer desired to
make the sound "ta" or "tu". The double tonguing is pronounced "ta ka" or "tu ku," while
the triple tongueing has the sound of "ta ta ka"

or "tu tu ku". These tonguings will be taken up later under the heading of "Exercises for Beginners".

Sustaining strength is acquired by the method of blowing. Some buglers puff out their cheeks and blow by sheer strength, which method will hardly permit the average man to play for any length of time. In practicing, the performer should hold the bugle with the two fingers of his right hand and learn to make his tones not through strength of blowing, but by the contraction of the lips, and in passing from one note to another the pressure should be the same, the change being made with the help of the muscles on the right and left of the lips or corners of the mouth. For the advise that these muscles should be massaged some cornet instructors have collected exorbitant fees.

The student is enjoined to always keep these requisites in mind, and to remember that a few minutes with a good, conscientious instructor is of much more value than hours of individual practice, as it is the constant cor-

rection that makes for proficiency: Errors
are more easily avoided than corrected.

If the student intends to read music, it will
be necessary before commencing with the
practice to learn something of the rudiments.
In this, as in blowing, the student will find
an instructor of great advantage, as it is difficult for an amateur to grasp the principles
without some aid and explanation.

RUDIMENTS OF MUSIC

Music is written on a staff, or a series of five equi-distant lines called leger lines (from the French "leger" or light, meaning lightly printed lines). The clef decides the names of the notes. The treble clef is used in bugle music and its C is between the 3rd and 4th lines from the bottom of the staff.

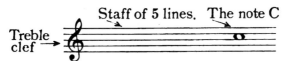

The value of notes and their corresponding rests is shown in the following illustration:-

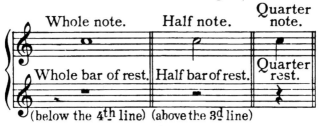

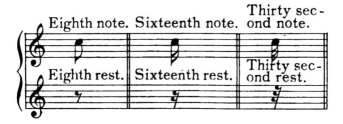

The whole note has no stem and is open. The half note is also open but has a stem, either upward or downward. The quarter note is a closed, or black note and has a stem. The eighth note is the same as the quarter, except that the stem has an additional tail, the 16th has two and the 32nd three of these tails.

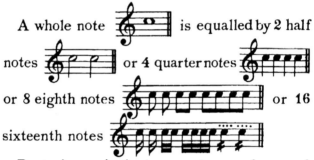

A whole note   is equalled by 2 half notes   or 4 quarter notes   or 8 eighth notes   or 16 sixteenth notes

Rests in equivalent amounts may be used instead of notes. The note C has been used exclusively but the above explanations are applicable to any note or combination of notes.

A dot placed after a note or rest increases its value or length by one half. A whole note followed by a dot   would be equal to six quarters instead of four, or three halves instead of two, thus:

A Half Note (or half rest) followed by a dot would be equal to three quarter notes or rests,

or their equivalents. 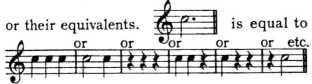 is equal to

The same rule applies to quarter notes, eighth notes etc. Should a note have two dots, which occasionally happens, the second dot would add one half of the value of the first dot.

The bar ▓ is indicated by a perpendicular line drawn across the staff, and its purpose is to divide the composition into e-qual parts, assisting to define the time.

At the end of a composition, or of an important section thereof, two thicker lines will

be found, and are called a Double Bar ▓

Every bar or measure is divisible into equal portions, called Beats, This subject is further mentioned in the chapter on Time.

Double dots adjacent to a double bar indi-cate that the strain toward which they face should be repeated, or played twice. The dots

are placed thus: ▓ or ▓

A Hold or Pause over a note

prolongs the note indefinitely, usually about three times its original length. In bugle music it is mostly used on the last note of a call or signal.

A Slur  is a

curved line drawn over or under two or more notes and ties them together into one continuous sound if the slurred notes are identical in pitch, as in the first bar above. When different notes are slurred, as in the other two examples, the sound or tone should glide from one to the other without the fresh attack of the tongue.

The figure three (*3*) over a group of notes signifies that three notes are to be played where, according to the division of the time two would have been written. The group is called a triplet and is written thus:

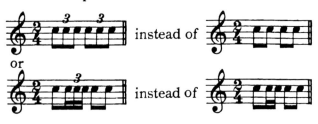

The converging lines above
or below a note or series of notes are called
(the first one) "crescendo" and (the second one)
"decrescendo". The crescendo gradually increases the volume of tone, the decrescendo
functioning in the opposite way.

The letters D. C. (Da Capo) at the end of
a composition indicate that the performer
should return to the beginning of the composition and play until the word "Fine"(Finish or
End) or the pause or hold ⌢ appears over
a double bar.

The Repeat bar ![repeat bar] means that the pre-
ceding bar should be played again, as if it
had been written twice.

TIME

There are several different kinds of time
and they are indicated immediately after the
clef mark. Outside of common time **C**, the
upper figure shows *how many* notes there
are to the bar, the lower figure showing *what
value* of notes.

Common Time, and Four Fourth time are
the same and are indicated by the sign **C**
and by the numerals $\frac{4}{4}$. Each bar contains
four quarters, or their equivalent. It is played

by counting four beats or steps.

Common time.

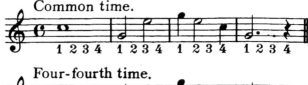

Four-fourth time.

When the Common Time indication has a line drawn through it, thus, ₵ the composition is played twice as quickly as otherwise. It is variously called "Alla Breve" Cut Time, "Half Time", etc. and one bar is played to two beats or steps instead of four.

Two-fourth time is composed of two quarters (or equivalent) and has two beats or steps to the bar. Example follows:

Six- eighth time is made of six eighth notes or the equivalent and is used at vari - ous rates of speed. If played in quick time or march time, it resolves itself into two beats or steps, each beat or step being equal to three eighths, as follows:

7

The upper figures denote the two beats in a bar. The lower figures count the eighths.

Three-fourth time is composed of three quarters (or equivalent) in each bar and has three counts or beats, thus:

Three-eighth time implies that in each bar there are three eighths. It is quite the same as three-fourth time.

EXERCISES
FOR BEGINNERS

The notes of a Bugle or Trumpet are as follows:

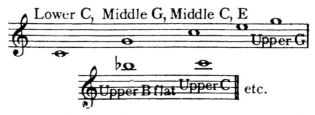

Lower C, Middle G, Middle C, E

Upper G

Upper B flat Upper C etc.

Only the first five of these notes are usually employed and they are easily learned by the positions they occupy on the staff. The lower C is written below the staff and has an added leger line drawn through it. Middle G is writ - ten on the second line from the bottom of the staff. Middle C is between the 3rd and 4th lines, E between the 4th and 5th lines, and upper G is just above the top line.

The middle G (next to lowest note) is the easiest note for the first practice. In blowing, place the tongue against the teeth, then imitate the pronunciation of the syllable "ta" or "tu", and in so doing, as the tongue with - draws, the air is precipitated into the ins - trument, causing the sound, The movement of the tongue is described as being similar to that of spitting a small hair from the tip.

The foregoing being understood, the student may now commence practicing the long
notes recommended for the development of
a good tone. Practice each one of the following notes many times before passing to
the next note. Do not leave a note until it
is mastered. Do not tire the lips too much
at first.

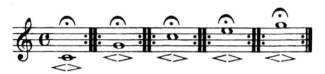

The following exercises in **C** Time (single
tonguing) may now be practiced. Do not try
to master them all at once. It is better to learn
one thoroughly than three indifferently.

IN COMMON TIME

IN THREE-FOURTH TIME

No. 17 and succeeding exercises will appear incomplete in the last bar, but the student will notice that in repeating the exercise the upbeat completes the bar.

IN TWO-FOURTH TIME

IN THREE-EIGHTH TIME

IN SIX-EIGHTH TIME
(two beats to a bar)

18

IN DOUBLE TONGUING

IN TRIPLE TONGUING

COMBINED TONGUING

FOR SUSTAINING STRENGTH
(see Instructions to Beginners)

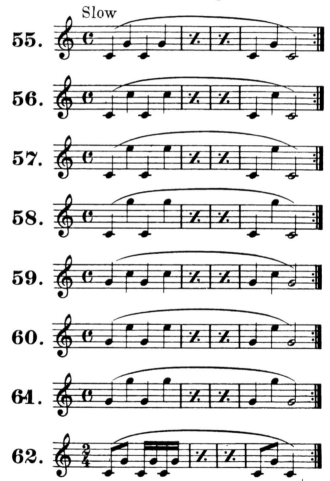

CLASSIFICATION OF CALLS

Warning Calls consist of First Call, Guard-mounting, Full Dress, Overcoats, Drill, Stable, Water, and Boots and Saddles. They precede Assembly by such interval as may be prescribed, these remarks applying in a general way to all branches of the Service.

Mess, Church and Fatigue, though classed as Service Calls, may also be used as Warning Calls.

First Call is the first signal for any formation implying roll call not otherwise provided for. Guardmounting and Drill calls show by their name to what use they are put.

Boots and Saddles is the signal for mounted formations, and immediately follows the call proper to the formation with which it is to be used. Full Dress and Overcoats follow the call with which they are to be used.

When buglers are united, they assemble at the first call pertaining to the formation.

Call to Quarters usually precedes Taps, and is the signal warning men to repair to their quarters.

Assembly is the signal for companies, troops or batteries to form on their parade grounds. Adjutant's Call is the signal for companies or guard details to form on the main parade ground, and usually follows Assembly. These two calls are known as Formation Calls.

Alarm Calls consist of Fire Call and To Arms, or To Horse, and both imply the least practicable delay. They are sounded by every trumpeter or bugler within hearing as quickly as possible, irrespective of time or place.

Service Calls consist of Tattoo,Taps,Mess, Sick, Church, Recall, Issue, Officers, Cap - tains, First Sergeants, Fatigue, School, Reveille, Retreat and the General. The latter is the signal for striking tents and loading wagons preparatory to marching. Reveille precedes the Assembly for roll call in the morning while Retreat follows the Assembly in the evening, the interval being that re - quired for formation and roll call, except when there is Parade.

Assembly, Reveille, Retreat, Adjutant's Call, To the Color, Flourishes and Marches are sounded by the united buglers. Tattoo may also be sounded by the united force while Assembly may be sounded by the musician of the Guard, according to the desire of the Commanding officer.

TIME OF CALLS

At daybreak, the hour and minute being specified in Post Orders, the Musician of the Guard sounds First Call. Ten or fifteen minutes later, as the Morning Gun is fired the assembled musicians play a march (if orders so specify), while the troops form before their barracks or tents. Reveille and Assembly are then sounded followed by a roll call of the troops, and reports by the ranking non-commissioned officers to the officer of the day, showing the organization present, or the amount of absentees.

One half hour later Mess Call is sounded by the Musician of the Guard. After breakfast, Stable Call, Water Call and Sick Call followed by Fatigue Call are sounded by the Musician of Guard at such hour and minute as Post Orders prescribe.

At times Drill, Parade and Guardmounting are held in the forenoon, at times in evening. Drill Call is sounded for Drill, First Call is sounded for Parade, and Guardmounting Call for Guardmount. Each of these are followed by Assembly in 10 or 15 minutes and by Adjutant's Call a few minutes later on Signal from the Adjutant. The Adjutant's Call is sounded for drill only when companies are combined into battalions. Recall is sounded at 11.30 A.M., First Sergeant's Call and Officers Call at 11.45 A.M. (but they may be sounded at any time of the day or night), and Mess Call at noon.

At one o'clock Fatigue Call is again sounded, followed by School Call, if required; Stable and Water Calls at 3.30, Recall at 4.30 or 4.00 according to the season.

First Call for Retreat (or Parade) is sounded just before sunset, or at such hour as the List of Calls directs, followed by Assembly and Retreat. After the formation (or before, according to season) Mess Call is again sounded. Tattoo at 9 P. M. Call to Quarters at 10.45 P.M. and Taps at 11.00 P. M.

DAILY BUGLE CALLS

1. First Call

Quick time.

2. Guard Mounting

Quick time.

3. Full Dress *(Dress Parade.)*
General Muster *(Navy)*

4. Overcoats.

5. Drill.

6. Stable. *(Army.)*
Saluting Gun Crews to Quarters. *(Navy.)*

7. Water.

8. Boots and Saddles.

9. Assembly. *(Army.)*
Division Call. *(Navy.)*

10. Adjutant's Call.

11. Fire.

Repeat at will

12. To Arms. *(Army.)*
Torpedo Defense Quarters *(Navy)*

Repeat at will

13. To Horse.

14. Reveille.

15. Retreat.
(All Buglers may play the 1st part.)

16. Tattoo
(usually sounded by one Bugler)

17. Call to Quarters.

18. Taps.

19. Mess. *(Army.)*
Spread Mess Gear. *(Navy.)*

20. Sick.

21. Church.

22. Recall.

23. Issue. *(Army.)*
Provision Call. *(Navy.)*

24. Officer's Call.

25. Captain's Call. *(Army.)*
Company Commanders. *(Navy.)*

26. First Sergeant's Call. *(Army.)*
Full Guard. *(Navy.)*

For Sergeant's Guard *(Navy)* sound only two bars.

27. Fatigue. *(Army.)*
Extra Duty. *(Navy.)*

28. School.

29. The General.

30. To the Color. To the Standard. *(Army.)*
Morning Colors. *(Navy.)*

Quick time

When there is no Band, this call, "To the Color," is sounded by the assembled Buglers in lieu of the Star-Spangled Banner immediately after the call "Retreat" has been sounded. During its performance the Garrison Flag is lowered, both at Retreat and Parade.

In the Navy, Morning Colors is sounded complete ashore, but aboard ship only the first half is played.

Should the Guard be turned out, the Musician of the Guard takes up a position three paces to the right of the Guard. If the Guard has been turned out on account of the approach of the National Colors, the first half of the above call "To the Color" is sounded immediately after the command "Present Arms". If the Guard has been turned out on account of the approach of some officer whose rank entitles him to a flourish or march, it is sounded immediately after arms have been presented to him.

MISCELLANEOUS CALLS.

31. President's March.

32. General's March. *(Army.)*
Commander in Chief. *(Navy.)*

33. Flourish for Review.

34. Rogues' March.

Repeat at will

35. Funeral March.

Repeat at will

36. Mail.

37. Hospital or Ambulance.

38. Boat. *(Army.)*

39. Liberty Party. *(Marine.)*

NAVY CALLS.

The Navy, as will have been noted, uses nearly the same calls as does the Army, with some exceptions. The following calls are used exclusively in the Navy:

40. General Quarters.

41. Secure.

42. Dismiss.

43. Clean Bright Work.

44 Put up Cleaning Gear,
or Knock off Bright Work.

45. Running Boat Crew

46. Away all Boats.

48

52. Carry On

53. Abandon Ship.

54. Swimming Call.

55. Go in the Water, or Overboard.

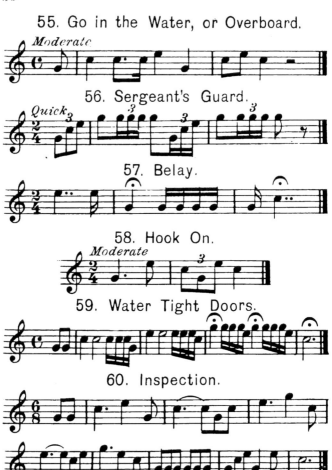

56. Sergeant's Guard.

57. Belay.

58. Hook On.

59. Water Tight Doors.

60. Inspection.

61. Light Smoking Lamp.

62. Out Smoking Lamp.

63. Torpedo Defense Fire Control Exercise.

64. Main Battery Fire Control Exercise.

65. Man Searchlights.

66. Man Range Finders.

67. Surgeon's Party

68. All Signalmen.

69. Working Party.

BOAT CALLS.
70. Steam Launches.

71. Cutters.

72. Whale Boat.

73. Barge.

74. Steamers.

75. Launches.

76. Race Boat Crew.

77. Gig.

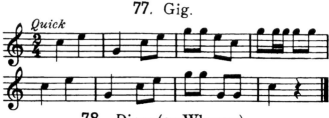

78. Dingy(or Wherry.)

To call away Dingy, sound this call twice, followed by one or two blasts.
To call away Wherry, sound this call once, followed by blasts if necessary.

CALLS FOR BOY SCOUTS.
79. Scouts' Call.

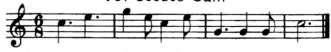

The above call is sounded before all of the reg-
ular calls and is intended to give notice that the
signal which follows is intended for the Scouts.
It is reproduced in this work by special permission of the Boy Scouts of America.

In addition to this, the following named Army Calls
are used by the Scouts, proficiency in which entitles the Scout to a merit badge.

Reveille, Mess Call, To the Color, Officer's
Call, Drill Call, Assembly, Recall, Fatigue,
Church Call, Fire Call, Swimming Call (see
Navy Calls), Retreat, Call to Quarters, and Taps.

DRILL SIGNALS.

At the end of many of the following signals the last note will be found repeated, after a pause. The second signal (Prepare to Mount), for instance, consists of two bars, the last note of which is G. These two bars mean "Prepare to Mount," while the repetition of the last note G afterwards means "Mount." In other words, "Prepare to Mount" is known as a preparatory command, while the additional "Mount" after a slight pause is the command of execution.

The memorizing of these signals will be greatly facilitated by observing that all movements to the Right are sounded on an ascending scale of notes while in the corresponding movements to the Left the descending progression is used.

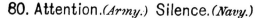

80. Attention. *(Army.)* **Silence.** *(Navy.)*

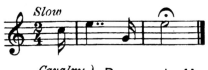

81. *Artillery (Drivers).* *Cavalry.* } **Prepare to Mount.**

82. *Cavalry.*
Artillery (Drivers). Prepare to Dismount.

83. *Artillery.* _ Cannoneers prepare to Mount.

84. *Artillery.* _ Cannoneers prepare to Dismount.

85. Forward. *(Army)*
Man the Drags. *(Navy)*

86. Halt.

87. Quick Time. *(Infantry.)*
(Cavalry and Artillery) Walk.

88. Double Time. *(Infantry.)*
Trot. *(Cavalry and Artillery.)*
Bear a Hand. *(Navy.)*

89. Galop. *(Cavalry and Artillery.)*

90. Charge. *(Army.)*
Man Overboard. *(Navy.)*

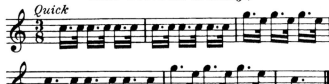

Repeat at will

91. Guide Right. *(Army.)*
Point Guns Forward. *(Navy.)*

92. Guide Left. *(Army.)*
Point Guns Aft. *(Navy.)*

93. Guide Centre. *(Army.)*
Point Guns Abeam. *(Navy.)*

58

94. *Cavalry.—*As Foragers.

95. *Artillery.—*Reverse.

96. *Artillery.—* Counter March.

97. Squads Right, or Sections *(Art.)* Right Turn.

98. Squads Left, or Sections *(Art.)* Left Turn.

99. Squads or Sections, Right About.

100. Squads or Sections,   Left About.

101. By the Right Flank. *(Army.)*
Sections Right Turn. *(Artillery.)*

102. By the Left Flank. *(Army.)*
Sections Left Turn. *(Artillery.)*

103. Column Right.

104. Column Left.

105. *Cavalry.* — Platoons.

106. Troops or Companies.

107. Squadrons or Battalions.

108. Cavalry. — Turn to the Right and Halt.
Infantry. — Company Right.
Artillery. — Platoons Right Turn.

109. Cavalry. — Turn to the Left and Halt.
Infantry. — Company Left.
Artillery. — Platoons Left Turn.

110. Right Turn.

111. Left Turn.

112. Right Oblique.

113. Left Oblique.

114. Guidons Out; or Guides Out.

115. Right Front into Line.

116. Left Front into Line.

117. Face to the Rear.

118. To the Rear, March.

119. *Infantry.* — To the Rear.

120. On Right into Line. *(Army.)*
Man Torpedo Defense Battery. *(Navy.)*

121. On Left into Line. *(Army.)*
Torpedo Defense Battery in Reserve. *(Navy.)*

122. Line of Platoons.

123. Line of Squads.

124. *Cavalry.*_Line of Fours.

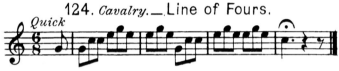

125. *Infantry.* _ Company Right Turn.
Artillery. _ Battery Right Wheel.

126. *Infantry.* _ Company Left Turn.
Artillery. _ Battery Left Wheel.

64

132. *Cavalry.* — To Fight on Foot.

133. Commence Firing.
Commence Coaling. (*Navy.*)

134. Cease Firing.
, Knock off Coaling. (*Navy.*)

135. Lie Down.

136. Rise, or Attention to Orders.

137. Route Step, or Route Order.

138. Fix Bayonets.

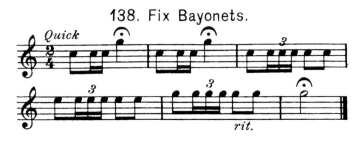

139. Pieces Front.

140. Caissons Front.

141. Double Section, Right Oblique.

142. Double Section, Left Oblique.

143. Flank Column, Right Oblique.

144. Flank Column, Left Oblique.

145. Right by Sections.

146. Left by Sections.

147. Form Double Section Line.

148. Form Rank or Posts

Moderate

149. Form Right Front into Echelon

Quick

150. Form Left Front into Echelon

Quick

QUICKSTEPS.

Marching Music (Quick time) is played at 120 beats or steps per minute, or one bar of two steps to the second.

Quickstep N⁰ 1, The First March.

Quickstep № 2, General Dooley.

Quickstep № 3, The Old Guard.

Quickstep No. 4, The American Flag.

Quickstep No. 5, The Cavaliers.

72

Quickstep N⁰ 6, Old Six-Eight.

Quickstep N⁰ 7, Infantry.

Quickstep N°8, The New Guard.

Quickstep N°9, I've got some years to do this in.

74

Quickstep № 10, Hens and Chickens.

Quickstep № 11, One, Two, Three.

Quickstep N⁰ 12, No Slum Today.

Quickstep N⁰ 13, Seventh Cavalry.

Quickstep N⁰ 14, The German Band.

Quickstep N⁰ 15, Oh, Look at the Soldiers.

Quickstep N⁰ 16, Get in Step.

Quickstep N⁰ 17, You're in the Army now.

Quickstep Nº 18, There She Goes.

Quickstep Nº 19, Old Du Pont.

Quickstep No 20, Happy Sam.

Quickstep No 21, Spanish Guardmount.

Quickstep N⁰ 22, Mexican Pete.

Quickstep N⁰ 23, The Red Hussars.

Quickstep № 24, The Firing Line.

Quickstep № 25, A hunting we will go.

Quickstep N⁰ 26, Drill Call March.

Quickstep N⁰ 27, Marching thru Georgia.

Quickstep № 28, Artillery.

Quickstep N.º 29, The Irish Soldier.

Quickstep N.º 30, Honolulu.

INSPECTION PIECES.

1. Old Knock Knees.

2. The Postilion.

3. Lieber Augustine.

86

4. Nick's Brother.

5. Austrian Tattoo.

6. The Tripler.

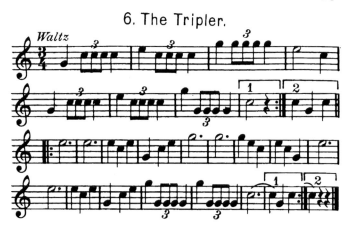

7. Montgomery Guards.

88

SOUND OFFS.

1. The Old One.

2. Holy Joe.

3. Soap Suds Row.

4. Slum and Duff Murphy.

5. Old Pompous.

6. Locker Pete.

7. General Burt.

DOUBLE TIME.
1. Pick it Up.

2. Pay Day.

3. Cavalry Trot.

BAND MARCH WITH B♭ BUGLE PARTS

American Trumpeter

MARCH

M. L. Lake.

HONORS

In the Navy, "Attention"or "Silence"is sounded previous to rendering further honors. This call is sounded in passing any ship entitled to a salute or when officers entitled to honors come aboard or depart.

The President will be received with the drums giving four ruffles and the bugles or trumpets sounding four flourishes followed by "To the Color" in the absence of a band.

An Ex-President and the Vice-President receive the same four ruffles and flourishes followed by a March in lieu of "To the Color."

The President of a foreign republic, a foreign sovereign or a member of a royal family – the four ruffles and four flourishes followed by the national anthem of his country.

A General receives four ruffles and flourishes followed by the General's March. A Lieutenant General receives three ruffles and flourishes followed by the General's March. A Major General receives two ruffles and flourishes followed by the General's March and a Brigadier General receives one ruffle and flourish followed by the General's March.

Cabinet Members, the Chief Justice, the President pro tempore of the Senate, the Speaker of the House of Representatives, American or foreign ambassadors and Governors within their respective States and Territories receive the same honors as the General, except that a foreign ambassador receives the national anthem of his country instead of the General's March.

The Assistant Secretary of War or Navy and American or foreign envoys or ministers receive the same as the Lieutenant General.

Officers of a foreign service receive honors due their rank.

Naval and Marine Officers are honored according to their relative rank with the above, as also Militia and Volunteer Officers when in the service of the United States.

"Taps" is sounded when a warship passes Washington's Grave at Mount Vernon between sunrise and sunset.

THE DRUM.

Music for the side or snare drum is usually written in the third or fourth space of the staff, thus: but it is immaterial on which space it is written, as there is no definite pitch for the drum.

Time, value of notes, rests and signs are the only necessities for the drummer to learn, all of which are found in the rudiments of music of this book.

There are also some abbreviations used in drum music which are applied to simplify writing for the drum. Explanations of those used in the United States Army tactics will be found at the beginning of the drum and fife signals. The others are, a half note which is marked thus: and should be played the same as four eighths, thus:

A quarter note marked thus: should be played the same as four sixteenths, thus:

A half note marked thus: should be played the same as eight sixteenths, thus:

Any note with three strokes, thus: is termed a roll, and should be continued as long as the value of the note.

Several notes tied together by a slur and three strokes across them, are known as a continuous roll, and are played the full value of the notes so tied together, thus:

The roll is the most difficult to perform of all drum-beats, and is the first thing that should be learned.

In beginning to learn the drum, the first essential to acquire is the position, which must be graceful, upright, but not too stiff. The heels should be placed together, the body erect, the drum slung so as to rest on the left thigh at such a height as to give pressure to the play of the sticks. The right hand stick should be held about two inches from the end, the thumb being well under. The left hand stick is held between the thumb and fore-finger, the butt end in the hollow passing between the second and third fingers, and resting on the first joint of the third finger; the fingers bending toward the palm of the hand.

The right elbow is kept almost close to the body; the left slightly raised, so that when the stick rests on the drum-head the arm will be in the form of a square.

Care should be taken that the sticks strike near the middle of the drum-head, and the wrists should not be held too stiff.

First, strike two taps with the left stick, then two with the right, repeating alternately, slowly and evenly, gradually increasing the time, each tap receiving the same force so that the sound will be of the same quality. This makes the open roll called by drummers the "Mammy-Daddy."

Every roll or beat should begin with the left hand, except those which are termed from hand to hand, which commence with the left and fol-low in succession.

Slightly accent the second stroke of each hand, and practice very slowly till perfect evenness is attained.

The letter L under a note is for the left hand, R is for the right, as per following examples:

The Open and Close Roll.

5.

These exercises should be practiced from two to five minutes at a time.

In the following exercise count four in each bar:

6.

The roll is very important in drum music and should be thoroughly learned; also practice the long roll by commencing very softly, gradually increasing to very loud.

The letter *p* is the abbreviation for *piano* and signifies soft, the letter *f* stands for *forte* and means loud.

7.

The Seven-stroke Roll, not being from hand to hand, must always begin with the left hand. The seventh stroke should be struck a little harder than the others, thus:

8.

The Five-stroke Roll is played from hand to hand, thus:

The Six-stroke Roll, thus:

The Eight-stroke Roll is from hand to hand, thus:

The Nine-stroke Roll is also from hand to hand, thus:

The Ten-stroke Roll, thus:

The Eleven-stroke Roll, thus:

L L R R L L R R L L R

The small notes, very often placed before the large notes, are called grace notes; they have no comparative value and do not change the time of the large notes before which they are played.

The flam beats employ the use of these small notes.

The Open Flam, thus:

L R   L R

The Close Flam. The two notes are sounded nearly as one and are from hand to hand, thus:

L R   L R   L R   L R

The close flam is used only in fast movements.

The Flam and Stroke, from hand to hand, is thus:

L R   L   R L   R

The Flam and Feint, from hand to hand, is thus:

The stroke should be the accented note.

The Feint and Flam is the previous example reversed, thus:

The Open Drag, thus:

The Close Drag or the Ruff, is thus:

The Single Drag is from hand to hand, thus:

The Double Drag is from hand to hand, thus:

The Single Ratamacue is from hand to hand, thus:

The Double Ratamacue is from hand to hand, thus:

The Treble Ratamacue is from hand to hand, thus:

The Four-stroke Ruff, is thus:

The Single Paradiddle is from hand to hand, thus:

These are very useful beats in quick movements.

The Flam Paradiddle is from hand to hand, thus:

The Stroke Paradiddle is from hand to hand, thus:

The strong accent is given on first note.

The Drag Paradiddle is from hand to hand, thus:

The Stroke and Drag Paradiddle is from hand to hand, thus:

The Stroke and Single Drag is from hand to hand, thus:

In the United States Army Calls, the figures placed under the notes indicate the number of strokes in each roll.

In band music the drummer must use his own judgment as to the number of strokes, according to the length of the notes, in slow or fast time.

Band music also has beats written on the unaccented part of a measure, called the up beats, and it is necessary to do this well to be a good band drummer. The best way to learn this is to beat the first and second parts of the bar with the foot and give the drum stroke between; the foot represents the part for the bass drum, which usually plays the down beats.

Exercises in Band Music.

Practice slowly at first, then increase to about the time of the quickstep.

Hail Columbia.

10. *Maestoso.*

The Red, White and Blue.

DRUM AND FIFE SIGNALS.

EXPLANATIONS.

A Ruffle is a short roll.

The Assembly repeated several times is given as the Fire Alarm.   The long roll is the signal "To Arms".

(t) indicates tap; (f), flam; (d), drag; (r), roll.   The figures under the rolls indicate the number of strokes in each roll.   Continuous roll,

The figures at the beginning of these signals indicate the time.   The General, for instance, is played so that 80 quarter notes will elapse in one minute.

1. The General.

2. The Assembly.

3. To the Color.

4. The Long Roll or to Arms.

5. The Reveille.

Go back to the first part of the Reveille.

6. Troop.

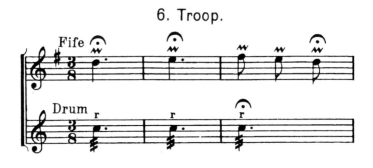

7. Retreat.

114

8. Tattoo.

After the three Rolls repeat Doubling to the End.

Play an Air in *Quick time*— after it, begin the Doubling.

Then an Air in *Common time*— after it, repeat the Doubling.

Then an Air in *Slow time*—and repeat the Doubling.

Finally an Air in *Double time,* followed by three Rolls.

MISCELLANEOUS INFORMATION
INSPECTION OF BUGLES

The inspecting officer draws sword and gives the command "Prepare for Inspection." He then returns sword or saber and inspects the organization, commencing on the right of the organization (his left).When he is approaching the bugler from the bugler's right, the lat - ter firmly grasps his 'instrument with the right hand and brings it up before his body at a height that brings his hand breast high, the bell of the instrument up, back of hand toward the inspector. As the latter is examining the instrument the bugler turns it so that all sides may be seen and then tips it, bell forward,so that the inside of the bell is visible.   As the inspecting officer passes on, the bugler returns the instrument to its position on his right hip.

POSTS OF MUSICIANS

In dismounted company formation the mu - sicians take position in the line of file closers in the first platoon, to the left of the 1st Lieutenant. When required to play they are posted at the head of the column. When the company is de - ployed,they accompany the captain, or company commander.

In cavalry, when mounted, one musician takes position one yard in rear and one yard to the left of the Captain or Troop Commander. When required to play, their position is at the head of the column as in dismounted organizations. On route marches the musicians take position between the Troop Commander and the first Squad. When there is a Squadron, one musician accompanies the Squadron Commander.

In Field Artillery when the battery is mounted, the musicians take a position boot to boot with each other, two yards in rear of the Captain or officer commanding the battery.

At Inspection the dismounted musicians take their usual position. In Cavalry (mounted) they take post two yards to the right of the right guide. In Field Artillery (mounted) boot to boot to the right of the guidon.

For "Retreat", musicians assemble at the flag staff immediately after "First Call" has been sounded.

When there is a band, the musicians fall in behind this organization and take position according to the number of bandmen in the rear rank, the object being to present a symmetrical formation. This applies to Guardmounting, Parade, Review, Escort of Colors, Funerals, Drills by Battalion or Squadron or Regiment and Street Parades. At these forma-tions they are required to sound "Adjutant's Call" when that officer draws his saber at the formation of the command. At Guardmounting, after the review the musicians turn out of column in the general direction of the guard house, and after the band has ceased playing they play marches or quicksteps on the way to the guard house. At Escort of Colors they sound "To the Color" at the command "Present Arms." At Reviews, should the Reviewing Officer be entitled to honors, they sound such flourish or march as is his due, once at the command "Present Arms" to him, and again while passing in review when the colors are lowered to him. In Street Parades they are sometimes required to relieve the Band by playing Quicksteps.

THE MUSICIAN OF THE GUARD.

The Sergeant Major details the Musician of the Guard by name on the guard detail for the day which is posted by the first sergeant on the bulletin board. He is liable to inspection the same as other members of the guard. He reports with the assembled musicians for guardmounting but on arriving at the guard house he takes post three paces to the right of the new guard where he remains until the usual courtesies have been paid. He then reports to the Adjutant as follows; "Sir, Musician John Smith (substitute real name) of C Company (substitute real name of company) reports as Musician of the Guard." He is then instructed to relieve the old musician of the guard, who informs him of any changes in orders or of any special orders.

He now consults the "List of Calls" and and sounds them at the hour and minute designated, and during the day remains at Headquarters, acting as orderly or messenger for the Adjutant. Should any formation be omitted on account of inclement weather he is instructed to sound the call corresponding to that formation, followed by "Recall." In sounding calls he first faces in one direction, sounding the call, then repeats it in the other direction so that all parts of the post will have the information clearly conveyed.

After supper he reports to the Guard House instead of the Adjutant's office, and takes all further orders from the Commander of the Guard, or higher authority. He remains at the Guard House over night and again reports to the Adjutant's office after "Sick Call."

While acting as orderly or messenger he must observe certain formulas that are customary. In carrying a verbal message from one officer to another he always prefaces it with the compliments of the sender. The Commanding Officer "directs"and the Adjutant "desires." For example, "The Commanding Officer's compliments to the Quartermaster and he directs the Quartermaster to report to him at Headquarters," or "The Adjutant's compliments, and desires to know if the Surgeon will examine this case." A musician answers an officer with "Yes, Sir" and "No, Sir" if this formula is sufficient, otherwise he adds whatever information he has to offer.

DAILY ROUTINE

Practice for buglers is designated at such hour in the morning that does not interfere with other company or troop duties, the time that the companies use for policing around the barracks being generally most convenient. Practice is in charge of the ranking man present, who designates what material shall be used for the drill. This is usually a matter of ten minutes of long tones blown at will by the individuals, followed by instruction in the Calls and Signals if required, the balance of the time being devoted to new marches or quicksteps, inspection pieces etc.

Whether all musicians should play both strains of a quickstep or whether an equal division should be made is a question that can only be decided upon the ranking man. As a matter of fact, it is not necessary for one half of the force to rest one half of the time, inasmuch as the performer does not need any more rest while blowing than is necessary to permit the circulation of the blood in the lips after the embouchure or lip is tired. This is only a matter of a bar or so.

Should there be no Band, the assembled buglers are required to take its place. They form at a distance of 30 paces on the right of the first company at parade. After "Adjutant's Call" they play a quickstep until the last company has halted on the line. At the command "Sound Off" they play suitable music. At the command "Officers front and center, March, Forward, MARCH,"they play a quickstep until either the officers have taken position in rear of the reviewing officer or have returned to their companies. At the command "Pass in Review" they at once make a turn to the right, and at the commands "Squads Right, MARCH"they march and play until the companies have left the parade ground.

At a Review the command is marched on the line the same as at parade. Later, when the reviewing officer comes within a short distance of the right of the line and turns, the buglers play appropriate marching music until he has again returned to the right of the line. The passing in review is the same as at parade except that the music ceases when the command has made and completed its second turn after having passed the reviewing officer.

The music stands fast until further commands are given. "Double Time" is played if the command is given; if not, the buglers join their companies for whatever ceremony may follow.

At Guardmounting Adjutant's Call is followed by a quickstep until the guard detail has halted on a line with the buglers. At the command "Prepare for Inspection" a suitable inspection piece is played until the Adjutant has inspected the rear of the second rank. Suitable music is played for "Sound Off" at the command, after which the guard is either marched in review as is the battalion at parade, or the order is given to march to its post. In review the music ceases when the guard passes the Officer of the Day, and after having turned out of the reviewing line, is taken up again at intervals on the way to the guard house. If the guard is marched to its post, the buglers turn in the general direction of the guard house (or as otherwise directed by the Adjutant) and at the command "March" play a short quickstep, then play others at intervals on the way, the same as at the review of the guard.

The so-called "Cheers" (the first "Sound -

Off." in this volume) may only be played *be-fore* and *after* another Sound-Off if the formation is a Morning Parade. If the parade is in the evening, after the music has terminated the Sound-Off, Retreat is sounded, followed by "To the Color" if there is no band present.

In the formation known as "Escort to the Color," or Standard, the command being formed, the Commanding Officer designates the company or troop that is to receive the Color. At this command the music moves forward without playing, and marks time until the escort arrives at its proper distance from the music, whether band or buglers, when the column moves at quick time to the Headquarters and is halted. At the command "Present Arms" the call "To The Color" is sounded. Appropriate commands are then given to bring the company on a line fifty paces in front of the battalion, music playing until the company halts. "To the Color" is again played at the repetition of the command "Present Arms," after which suitable commands are given to march the company to the right, then in rear of the battalion and to its original place, the music playing from the time the movement is executed to the right, ceasing when the company is well past the line of the battalion, the music, though not playing, continues to march until it has regained its original position on the right of the battalion.

For Funeral Ceremonies, the Musician of the Guard is instructed to sound "Church Call" followed by "Assembly". The music and troops form at the Hospital or other desig - nated place. When the body is borne out, the commander of the firing squad gives the command "Present Arms" while suitable music is played. If the deceased is entitled to a flour- ish or march, it is sounded at that command. The procession is headed by the music, fol - lowed by the escort, or firing squad, to which is attached the bugler who later sounds "Taps". Having arrived at the destination, the coffin is carried along the front of the escort to either the grave or train, the music playing mean- while, but ceases when the coffin has been placed over the grave or other place of rest. After a volley has been fired, the bugler sounds

"Taps" and the command marches homeward, no music being played until the troops have left the cemetery or a reasonable distance from the railroad depot.

BUGLE SIGNALS

The following Bugle Signals may be used off the battlefield when not likely to convey information to the enemy;

Attention. Troops are brought to attention.

Attention to Orders. Troops fix their attention.

Forward, March. Used also to execute quick time from double time.

Double Time, March.

To the Rear, March. In close order execute *Squads Right About.*

Halt.

Assemble, March.

The following bugle signals may be used on the battlefield.

Fix Bayonets.

Charge.

Assemble, March.

These signals are used only when intended

for the firing line; hence they can only be authorized by the commander of a unit (Regiment or brigade) which occupies a distinct section of the battlefield.

The following bugle signals are used in exceptional cases on the battlefield. Their principal uses are in field exercises and practice firing;

Commence Firing. Officers charged with fire direction and control open fire as soon as practicable. When given to a firing line the signal is equivalent to *Fire at Will.*

Cease Firing. All parts of the firing line execute *cease firing* at once.

These signals are not used by units smaller than a regiment except when such unit is independent or detached from its regiment.

Buglers of the Engineer Corps, Signal Corps and Hospital Corps perform the same duties as required of Infantry buglers when dismounted, and of Cavalry buglers when mounted. Infantry regulations and customs also prevail in the Coast Artillery as far as the bugler and calls are concerned. The Marine Corps conforms to the Navy calls as also does the Revenue Service.

BUGLE SPECIFICATIONS

The following are the Specifications for the
manufacture of the B♭ Bugle as published by
the Quartermaster Department of the Army.

To be made of what is known as "Special
first-class quality trumpet brass", twenty-three
gauge, strengthened at the outer edge of bell
by three-sixteenths of an inch solid, half-round
brass wire. To have two brass rings of No. 8
U. S. standard gauge wire, with one-half an
inch opening, secured to three-quarter inch
circular plates soldered on for the sling strap,
one at the inner portion of the top bend, and
the other on the inner portion of the lower
bend.

The mouth-ferrule to be of double thickness
of tubing, about one inch long, fitting exactly
the taper of the mouthpiece shank. To have a
brass ferrule in center of each of the three back
bends, about three-fourths of an inch long, fitting exactly the tubing of the bugle, to which
it should be securely soldered. The bell portion to be of the best hammered brass. A loose
attaching link to neck of mouthpiece formed

of No. 13 German silver wire, outer portion of link twisted 90 degrees to form a "D" toward lip-piece; loose ends of wire forming this link to be brought together and silver soldered.

Each bugle and mouthpiece to weigh about eleven and three-fourths ounces. The diameter of the bell to be about three and five-eighths inches; the extreme length to be about eight inches, not including mouthpiece; extreme width to be about four inches.

Each bugle to be built in the key of B-flat and made on the prototype system in order to insure a perfect quality of tone.

Finish: Entire outer surface of both bugle and mouthpiece to be finished by sand-blasting. Finish interior of bell portion to the depth of three inches, to be also sand-blasted. Entire surface to be finished by sand-blasting, to be lacquered with transparent lacquer.

Sling: The sling to be made in two parts from russet collar leather. It consists of a one-half inch piece, fifteen inches long, over all, trimmed with a loose one-half inch bridle buckle attached to free end by an attaching button and sliding loop. Second piece is one-half inch

by forty-two and one-fourth inches over all, is
tapered and has six tongue-holes punched one
inch apart, beginning two and one-fourth inches from tapered end. Both pieces are attached
to their respective metal loops on bugle by a
three-eighths inch leather loop.

Strap: The mouthpiece strap to be made
of same leather as sling, three-eighths inch
wide, seven and three-fourths inches long over
all; trimmings with bar buckle at one end, with
a three-eighths inch leather loop on reverse
side. Opposite end is tapered and punched
with three tongue-holes at one-fourth inch cen-
ters, commencing at one inch from tapered end,
the strap to be attached by means of a leather
loop and is then buckled through the attaching link on the mouthpiece.

In all points not covered by these specifications to be like and equal to the standard
sample in all respects.

FLAG SIGNALS

The signal flags described below are car -
ried by the company musicians in the field.

1st Battalion; Company A, red field, white square
　　　　　　　Company B, red field, blue square
　　　　　　　Company C, red field, white diagonals
　　　　　　　Company D, red field, blue diagonals

2nd Battalion; Company E, white field, red square
　　　　　　　Company F, white field, blue square
　　　　　　　Company G, white field, red diagonals
　　　　　　　Company H, white field, blue diagonals

3rd Battalion; Company I, blue field, red square
　　　　　　　Company K, blue field, white square
　　　　　　　Company L, blue field, red diagonals
　　　　　　　Company M, blue field, white diagonals

In addition to their use in visual signalling,
these flags serve to mark the assembly point
of the company when disorganized by combat,
and to mark the location of the company in bi-
vouac and elsewhere, when such use is desirable.

In a regiment in which it is impracticable to
make the permanent battalion division alphabetically, the flags of a battalion are as shown; flags
are assigned to the companies alphabetically within their respective battalions, in the order given above.

The General Service Code (explained later) is used for all signals not otherwise provided for. The Dot is executed by a motion to the right, the Dash to the left. The Dot embraces an arc of 90 degrees, or a quarter circle, starting with the vertical and returning to it, and is made in a plane at right angles to the line connecting the stations. The Dash to the left conforms in all other particulars to the foregoing instruct - ions. The Pause is executed with a motion to the front, downward, directly in front of the sender, the flag being afterwards instantly re- turned to its original position, that is, flag held vertically, the sender facing the other commun- icating station.

A light colored flag shows best on a dark back- ground and vice versa. Keep the hands apart and describe a circle in each movement to the right or left. Care should be taken that letters are sent distinctly and not jumbled. Spell all numerals and do not abbreviate words that are written out.

The General Service Code may also be trans- mitted on the bugle, whistle or drum. A short note on C indicating a Dot, a long note indi- cating Dash, and a note on G representing end of letter or figure. The end of word and sentence may be represented by longer blasts on other notes such as lower C or upper G, according to any previous un- derstanding.

THE GENERAL SERVICE CODE.

A .—	H	O ———	V ...—
B —...	I ..	P .——.	W.——
C —.—.	J .———	Q ——.—	X —..—
D —..	K —.—	R .—.	Y —.——
E .	L .—..	S ...	Z ——..
F ..—.	M ——	T —	
G ——.	N —.	U ..—	

NUMERALS.

1 .————	6 —....
2 ..———	7 ——...
3 ...——	8 ———..
4 ....—	9 ————.
5	0 —————

PUNCTUATION.

Period .. .. ..
Comma .—.—.—
Interrogation ..——..
Hyphen —....—
Parentheses —.—.—.—
Quotation Marks .—..—.
Bar indicating fraction —..—.
Underline ..——.— (before and after words un-
                        derlined.)
Double dash —...—
Cross .—.—.
Exclamation ——..——
Apostrophe .————.
Semicolon —.—.—.
Colon ———...

CONVENTIONAL SIGNS.

End of word: Front.

End of sentence: Front, front.

End of message: Front, front, front.

Error: A. A. front.

Acknowledgment: M. M. front.

Cease signalling: M. M. M. front.

Repeat after (word): C. C. front, A. front (word).

Repeat last word: C. C. front, front.

Repeat last message: C. C. C. front, front, front.

Move a little to the right: R. R. front.

Move a little to the left: L. L. front.

Move a little uphill: U. U. front.

Move a little downhill: D. D. front.

Signal faster: F. F. front.

Wait a moment: . _ . . . front.

Signature follows: Sig. front.

Officers, platoon leaders, guides and musicians are equipped with whistles. Guides and musicians assist by repeating signals when necessary. Battalion and company commanders use a whistle of different tone than that of the whistle used by platoon leaders, guides and musicians.

For communication between the firing line and reserve, or commander in rear, the subjoined signals (Signal Corps code) are pre-scribed and should be memorized. In trans-mission, their concealment from the enemy's view should be insured. In the absence of signal flags, the headdress or other substitute may be used. After dark a lantern or other light may be used, providing another light is placed at the sender's feet as a guide.

Letter of alphabet.	If signaled from the rear to the firing line.	If signaled from the firing line to the rear.
A M ..	Ammunition going forward	Ammunition required.
C C C ..	Charge (mandatory at all times).........	Am about to charge if no instructions to the contrary.
C F . . .	Cease firing	Cease firing.
D T. . . .	Double time or "rush". .	Double time or "rush".
F.	Commence firing.	
F B . . .	Fix bayonets.	
G.	Move forward	Preparing to move forward
H H H. .	Halt.	
K	Negative	Negative.
L T . . .	Left.	Left.
O	What is the (R N, etc.)?.	What is the (R N, etc.)?
P	Affirmative	Affirmative.
R N. . .	Range.	Range.
R T. . .	Right	Right.
S S S . .	Support going forward.	Support needed.
S U F . .	Suspend firing. . . . . :	Suspend firing.
T	Target . . . . : .	Target.

MISCELLANEOUS SIGNALING.

Other systems include the Flashing or Occult Light System as used in the Navy. In this, a short flash represents a Dot, a longer flash the Dash, and a much longer flash the Pause. These flashes are made either with a searchlight or a covered side light. The Navy also uses the Bugle System as already described - short note for Dot, longer note for dash, etc. In the Ardois System a red light represents the Dot and a white light the Dash. End of word is represented by the letters RW.

THE PISTOL.

The automatic pistol calibre .45, model of 1911 in the military service has three principal parts: the receiver, the barrel and the slide. It has a hollow handle into which the magazine is inserted from below and locked in place by the magazine catch. The magazine may be re - moved by pressure upon the checkered end of the magazine catch which projects from the left side of the receiver in a convenient posi- tion for operation by the thumb.

The barrel is largest at the breech, and at the top has two transverse locking ribs. The rear end of the barrel is attached to the receiver by the link, link pin and the pin of the slide stop.

When the slide is in its forward position and the hammer is full cocked, the safety lock may be pushed up manually, by means of the thumb piece, thereby positively locking the hammer and the slide. If the safety lock is pressed down so as to release the slide, the projecting stud on the safety lock clears the sear, permitting the sear to be operated by the trigger, thereby causing the release of the hammer if the grip safety is pressed inward, as by the hand grasping the handle of the pistol, then the trigger may be pulled.

OPERATION.

A loaded magazine is placed in the handle and the slide drawn fully back and released, thus bringing the first cartridge into the chamber. The hammer is thus cocked and the pistol is ready for firing.

For firing the maximum number of shots, draw back the slide, insert a cartridge by hand into the chamber of the barrel, allow the slide to close, then lock the slide and the cocked hammer by pressing the safety lock upward, and insert a loaded magazine. The slide and hammer being thus positively locked, the pistol may be carried safely at full cock, and it is only necessary to press down the safety lock (at the thumb) when raising the pistol to the firing position.

MEMORANDA.

Never place the finger within the trigger guard until it is intended to fire.

Keep the pistol cleaned and oiled. Excessive oiling causes the parts to gum and work stiffly.

Take care in inserting the magazine that it engages with the magazine catch.

Pressure must be entirely relieved from the trigger after each shot, that the trigger may re-engage with the sear.

To remove cartridges not fired, disengage the magazine slightly and extract the cartridge in the barrel by drawing back the slide.

Don't snap the hammer when the pistol is partially disassembled.

Before loading, draw back the slide and look through the bore to see that it is free from obstruction.

The trigger must be pulled to fire each separate shot. The automatic action ejects the empty shell, forces another cartridge into place and cocks the pistol for the next shot.

PISTOL MANUAL.

The instruction under this head is first given on foot. When a lanyard is used, one end is attached to the butt of the pistol, the other end forms a sliding loop which is passed over the head and drawn snug against the right armpit. The lanyard should then be of just such length that the arm can be extended without constraint.

The pistol being in the holster, to raise pistol the command is given *1. Raise, 2. Pistol.*

At the command *Raise*, unbutton the holster flap with the right hand and grasp the stock back of the hand to the body. At the command *Pistol* draw the pistol from the holster, reverse it, muzzle up, the hand holding the stock with the thumb and last three fingers; the little finger may be placed under the butt; forefinger outside of the guard, guard to the front, barrel nearly vertical; hand as high as the neck and six inches to the right and front of the right shoulder. This is the position of *Raise, Pistol.*

Being at Raise Pistol: *1. Return, 2. Pistol.*

Insert the pistol in the holster, back of hand to the body, button the flap and drop the hand by the side.

1. Inspection, 2. Pistol.

Execute raise pistol, except that the pistol is held about six inches in front of the center of the body, barrel up, pointing to the left front and upward at an angle of about 45 degrees, wrist straight and as high as the breast. Cart-ridge boxes, if worn, are then opened with the left hand.

The inspector passes along the rank and ex-amines the pistols and cartridge boxes; each box is closed as soon as inspected. To inspect the pistol minutely, he takes it in his hands and then returns it to the soldier, who grasps it at the stock and resumes *Inspection Pistol:* each man returns pistol as the inspector passes to the next. If the pistols are not inspected, they are returned by the commands: *1. Return, 2. Pistol.*

For the purposes of instruction the men may be required to execute Inspection Pistol sim-ultaneously, suitable caution being given to that effect by the instructor. But at formal in-spections, the men execute *Inspection Pistol* in succession as the inspector approaches them.

WORDS TO BUGLE CALLS.

Printed by kind permission of Elbert Williams
(late Principal Musician, 9th Cavalry Band.)

FIRST CALL.

Rally ye horn skilled Buglers
Cold chilled Trumpeters
Field music all,
Others take care
That you repair
Ready where
You answer to First Call.

GUARD MOUNTING.

Outside all the new guards have your equip-
ments shining and bright,
First Sergeants are quite close inspectors
for they know every slight,
To make orderly's hard for you have to be
clean and drill right,
The adjutant's called odd if he gives two a
sight.

FULL DRESS.

Now put on your full dress;
Full uniforms impress;
Put on full dress.

OVERCOATS.

Overcoats, Overcoats, Overcoats.

DRILL.

Get them out Corporal Krout,
If you can't get them out,
Then put them in the mill;
Get them out at a rout,
Get them out with a shout,
Outside you soldiers for drill.

STABLE.

March over to the stable
And groom lively if you're able,
And feed all your noble horses on corn nice
clean oats and hay;
Give some grain to the white and give some
grain to the gray,
Give some grain to the black and give some
grain to the bay,
March over from the stable
Repair clean washed to the table,
And eat heartily and drink while you feel
inclined that way.

WATER.

Water your horses how plain the trumpet calls.

BOOTS AND SADDLES.

Go to your horses
Bridle and saddle them up
Surcingles cinchas on them all.

ASSEMBLY.

When the trumpet sounds this call,
Every soldier has to fall,
In the front rank or rear,
And when called answer "here."

ADJUTANT'S CALL.

Winter or spring summer or fall,
This is the sound of Adjutant's call,
Winter or spring summer or fall,
This is the sound of Adjutant's call.

TO THE STANDARD.

To the Standard or Color whenever uncased,
As it passes a party that arms bear;
The salute as prescribed will be made with
     good taste,
While the field music is sounding quick this
     martial fanfare,
Tis our flag we'll never let it drag,
We'll never from it lag,
We love the pretty flag of liberty, flag of
     liberty,
Flag of our country free.

FIRE.

To the fire,
To the fire
Go to the fire, take the double time
And if you go a bit too slow,
Or soon begin to tire,
Sarge in charge will fuss you know,
Because you'll rise his ire.

TO ARMS.

To Arms, To Arms;
Get your guns, get your guns,
Get your guns, get your guns,
Get them from the stacks,
Get them from the racks.

TO HORSE.

Go to the picket line and get your horse,
You are to get him where'er he may be of course

REVEILLE.

All out do you hear
All be of good cheer
All wash and see clear
Stop yawning,
All hurry and dress
All make a rough guess
All say what's for mess
This morn.
This means the Captain's flunky
The men on pass and bunky
And others need not monkey
For reveille's half gone.

RETREAT.

Day's o'er and eve
Now is our guest,
The sun must leave
To go down in the west,
Let the soldiers off from duty be:
They like to go to see their girls you know,
Some get dry, and drink rye
Others take in every show
To which they have the price to go.

TATTOO.

Tattoo used to be a bedtime roll call
Sounded by trumpeters many,
Long before the birth of call to quarters
The music was scored for trumpeters three
At the hour of nine
They would fall into line
And the notes of this fanfare
They'd sound superfine.
Come on soldiers dont lag behind
If you do surely you will get a five dollar blind.
With blinds went confinement
And plenty of work to do
A Sentry with rifle behind you;
All who came this call to attend
Were reported as present and were wise in the end;
Tattoo, Tattoo, Answer and to bed you.

CALL TO QUARTERS.

Time to rest,
The trumpet sounds call to quarters;
Bear in mind while so inclined,
If you're behind you'll get a blind.
Say my love true
I must skidoo,
Time to rest.

TAPS.

Go to sleep, peaceful sleep,
May the soldier or sailor God keep,
On the land or the deep
Safe in sleep.

MESS.

Recruits and old soldiers
Chow call in the service means
Come and get your coffee
Bread bacon and army beans
And some may get plum duff,
Bunk fatigue and pipe dream scenes.

SICK.

Call for the sick,
Crutch hops walk funny,
Go tell to the Doctor your ills,
He'll treat your case,
And without money,
For Uncle Sam pays all the bills, the bills,
        the bills.

CHURCH.

Go to church if you care,
Do the right if you dare.
Some folks go to church to sing and pray
Others to hear the Preacher's say,
Many for they were raised that way,
Go, all are welcome there.

RECALL.

Recall is a call that never was invented
For those who always shirk
Recall is a call that ever means rest
Unto the ones that work.

ISSUE.

Issue to those who a known quantity of ra-
        tions are free,
Issue to those too that draw from the Q. M. D.

OFFICER'S CALL.

Young Officers old officers Field Officers all,
You're ordered to headquarters by officers' call.

CAPTAIN'S CALL.

Come officers some officers not officers all
Hear the Captain's call.

FIRST SERGEANT'S CALL.

First Sergeant's or orderly call
Tops lean or fat, long short and tall
Get your reports, orders for all.

FATIGUE.

Jones take that old shovel or pick
Smith use that hoe,
Brown grab that new wheelbarrow quick,
Dont work too slow.
Fatigue call's no grand thing at all
I'll let you know;
Says Sergeant the Provo.

SCHOOL.

Go to school lads,
Go to school dads;
If you want a raise in rank
Which carries better pay,
You should try to get wise
Each and every day.

THE GENERAL.

Hark! this is the gen'ral going,
Mark! long as the trumpets blowing,
There ought to be tents up showing tent
    flies;
First look at the tents all standing,
Then see all the squad chiefs planning
And most of the soldiers manning tent
    guys;
Hear some Lance Jack calling
You! Mack put those wall pins in that
    sack,
And move that tripod nearer the back;
Keep your tents from falling,
Hold the guys loose the flies
Dont let her fall
Until the last note of the call;
Get ready one and all;
All ready let her fall.

THE NINTH CAVALRY TROT DOUBLE TIME.

We're the men that fought at Wounded Knee,
Troopers of the brave Ninth Cavalry.
Straight up in the saddle troopers
Trot your horses with pride;
One two three four, That's the way to ride.

THE NINTH CAVALRY CALLOP.

In hot or cold weather we move out together,
We gallop our horses and sing merrily,
With hearts stout as leather and light as a
    feather,
We follow the flag of the Ninth Cavalry,
Straight up in the saddle troopers all ride
    straddle
With spurs on their heels and reins in their
    left hand,
We gather our horses and make them skedaddle
When gallop is heard as our Co'nels command.

OTHER WORDS
TO BUGLE CALLS.

REVEILLE.

I can't get 'em up, I can't get 'em up,
I can't get 'em up in the morning
I can't get 'em up, I can't get 'em up,
I can't get 'em up at all.
    Get up you sleepy monkeys,
    And wake up your lazy bunkies,
    Put on your working breeches,
    And go out and do your work,
I can't get 'em up, I can't get 'em up,
I can't get 'em up in the morning
I can't get 'em up, I can't get 'em up,
I can't get 'em up at all.

MESS CALL.

Soupy, Soupy, Soupy, without a single bean,
Coffee, coffee, coffee, without a bit of cream,
Porky, porky, porky, without a bit of lean.

STABLE CALL.

Come all who are able and go to the stable,
Want water your horses and give 'em some corn,
For if you don't do it, the Col'nel will know it,
And then you will rue it, as sure as you're born,
So come to the stable, all ye who are able and
Water your horses and give 'em some corn.

TAPS.

1.

Love, good night,
Must thou go,
When the day
And the night
Need thee so?
All is well.
Speedeth all
To their rest.

2.

Fades the light;
And afar
Goeth day,
And the stars
Shineth bright,
Fare thee well;
Day has gone,
Night is on.

TRUMPET CORDS *(Illustrated)*

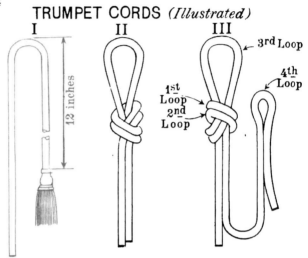

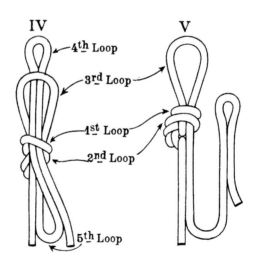

VI

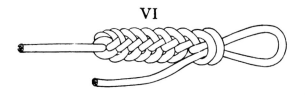

VII

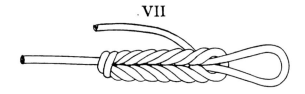

VIII

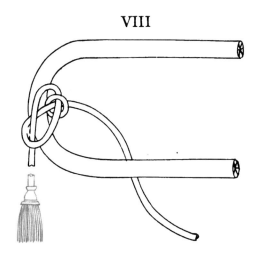

TRUMPET CORDS
and how to braid them.

An essential accessory to the trumpet is the cord, and as in commands where Trumpets are still used, regulations require that the braiding be done in a specified manner, the following instructions are appended.

The Trumpet cord according to regulation is several feet in length and has a tassel at each end.

What is known as "Triple Braiding" is most popular and best appearing, and is the form that will be described here.

To "Triple Braid", bend the cord in a loop, *(as in figure I)* about 12 inches from the tassel. Then hold the two cords below the loop and make an ordinary knot, *(See figure II)*

Then reverse, holding the knot in the left hand, and the main cord in the right; make a loop (4th loop) with the right hand, *(See fig - ure III)* insert it between the 1st and 2nd loops, and then pull it through the 3rd loop *(See figure IV)*.

Hold loop 4 *(See figure IV)* in the right hand and pull taut which will take up the slack in the 3rd and 5th loops. This will make the 4th loop too large, so pull on the right hand cord until the 4th loop acquires the desired size.

It may be necessay when starting the braid to work the 3rd loop down against the 1st loop by pulling and tightening at the other loops.

If this has been done for an inch or so, it only becomes necessary to pull the 4th loop taut, which will cause the 3rd loop to come down in contact with the 1st loop.

When the 3rd loop has been pulled down against the 1st loop, another loop is made with the right hand *(See figure V)* and is inserted between the 1st and 2nd loops and then pulled through the 3rd loop, following the same process as in figure IV.

This is repeated until the braiding is as long as is required. Allowance should be made that several inches are left at each end, that the cord may be fastened to the trumpet.

Figure VI shows a part of the completed braid on the front or "triple" side. Figure VII shows how it appears on the opposite or reverse side.

Figure VIII shows how the ends of the cord are fastened to the trumpet.

Damp weather sometimes causes the cord to shrink and thereby often causes the braided portion to warp. For this reason loops should not be pulled too tightly.

When the braiding has reached the desired length, the tassel should be inserted through the last loop (loop 3) and the cord drawn tight.

THE
AMATEUR
BAND GUIDE
AND AID TO LEADERS.

*A Reference Book for All Wind Instrument Players
Describing
the construction and maintainance of Bands, their
organization, instrumentation and all other complete information that is necessary or desirable.*

by *EDWIN FRANKO GOLDMAN*

The object of this little volume is to provide for Band-
masters, Band Teachers, and Bandsmen in general a hand-
book which will prove of value in the organizing and proper
maintaining of Bands. Designed primarily for the purpose of
giving advice, information and suggestions for young bands,
the book contains many points which may well prove of advantage and interest to older and more experienced players.

The Bandmaster will find use for this book, for in it his
position and work are explained fully and in detail. Wind
Instrument players will find use for it because, aside from
describing the entire workings of a band, it offers suggestions for the care of instruments, how and what to practice,
methods and studies which should be familiarized, a descrip-
tion of each Band instrument, showing its compass and
possibilities, etc., etc.

The Book also contains charts showing correct seating
of bands for concert purposes, proper formations for marching, instrumentation of bands, of from ten to one hundred
men, a chart for tuning purposes, a revised constitution
and by-laws, rules and regulations governing band contests,
and other subjects too numerous to mention here.

PRICE: $1. 50 in U. S. A.